797,885 Books
are available to read at

Forgotten Books

www.ForgottenBooks.com

Forgotten Books' App
Available for mobile, tablet & eReader

ISBN 978-1-330-82038-4
PIBN 10109678

This book is a reproduction of an important historical work. Forgotten Books uses state-of-the-art technology to digitally reconstruct the work, preserving the original format whilst repairing imperfections present in the aged copy. In rare cases, an imperfection in the original, such as a blemish or missing page, may be replicated in our edition. We do, however, repair the vast majority of imperfections successfully; any imperfections that remain are intentionally left to preserve the state of such historical works.

Forgotten Books is a registered trademark of FB &c Ltd.
Copyright © 2017 FB &c Ltd.
FB &c Ltd, Dalton House, 60 Windsor Avenue, London, SW19 2RR.
Company number 08720141. Registered in England and Wales.

For support please visit www.forgottenbooks.com

1 MONTH OF FREE READING

at

www.ForgottenBooks.com

By purchasing this book you are eligible for one month membership to ForgottenBooks.com, giving you unlimited access to our entire collection of over 700,000 titles via our web site and mobile apps.

To claim your free month visit: www.forgottenbooks.com/free109678

* Offer is valid for 45 days from date of purchase. Terms and conditions apply.

English
Français
Deutsche
Italiano
Español
Português

www.forgottenbooks.com

Mythology Photography **Fiction**
Fishing Christianity **Art** Cooking
Essays Buddhism Freemasonry
Medicine **Biology** Music **Ancient Egypt** Evolution Carpentry Physics
Dance Geology **Mathematics** Fitness
Shakespeare **Folklore** Yoga Marketing
Confidence Immortality Biographies
Poetry **Psychology** Witchcraft
Electronics Chemistry History **Law**
Accounting **Philosophy** Anthropology
Alchemy Drama Quantum Mechanics
Atheism Sexual Health **Ancient History**
Entrepreneurship Languages Sport
Paleontology Needlework Islam
Metaphysics Investment Archaeology
Parenting Statistics Criminology
Motivational

A HISTORY OF
THE VERNON HOUSE

IN NEWPORT, R. I.

❧

BY
MAUD LYMAN STEVENS

PUBLISHED BY
THE CHARITY ORGANIZATION SOCIETY
OF NEWPORT, THE PRESENT OWNERS
1915

COPYRIGHT 1915
BY
MAUD LYMAN STEVENS

THE VERNON HOUSE

There stands in the ancient town of Newport, on the Island of Rhode Island, a house of unusual historic interest. This house has recently been purchased under circumstances which ensure its permanent preservation. It is therefore now entitled to a review of its past, and it has been thought that it would be agreeable and fitting at this time, to consider, somewhat in detail, the scenes that it has witnessed and the distinguished persons who have been entertained within its walls. To such a retrospect, this paper is dedicated.

The State of Rhode Island and Providence Plantations, to give it its full title, is the smallest in the Union. It is, nevertheless, as its name indicates, made up of two very distinct parts. Two capitals, persisting to modern times, long reminded us of this dual origin. Providence was founded by the Salem minister, Roger Williams; Rhode Island by a body of men from Massachusetts Bay who differed from the Puritan tenets, and desired liberty of conscience. With this in view, they came hither to found in the wilderness a state, in which, following the inner light, they might also assure to others the freedom which they had been denied.

The first settlement on this island was made in 1638. Newport was founded in the following year—May, 1639. Of the nine adventurers who were banded together in this enterprise, one is of special interest to us, for it is on his original grant that the "Vernon House" stands.

Jeremy Clarke was his name, and the tract of land apportioned to him was a choice one. Extending, it is said, from the Parade to Church Street, and from the waterside to a line high on the hill, it covered a number of acres of most desirable land, high and well drained, as well as convenient to the centre of the town.

Jeremy Clarke's house stood, it is believed, just above the line of the present Thames Street. With the green plot before it and the water beyond—behind, the orchard and fields—it must have been a pleasant place of residence. Living and dying here, Jeremy Clarke was buried on his own land, in a tomb by the waterside, the site of which is long since obliterated. To him succeeded his son, Walter Clarke, the Governor, and he it was who divided the land, running a street through it from East to West—called New Lane or Mary Street, the last name traditionally for his wife, Mary. Another street, starting from the Parade and bounding Walter Clarke's orchard, was and is called Clarke Street.

At the north-east corner of these two streets, stands the old house with which we are concerned. At this point we find ourselves among uncertainties. Divided among various Clarke heirs, this part of the land passed out of the family's hands, though when we do not know. The fragmentary condition of the Newport town records makes research into early conditions here very difficult. It is said that there was an earlier house on this site, as the present timbers bear signs of reworking, and the name of William Gardner has been mentioned in connection with it—a Narragansett man, who died at sea in 1727. The first definite fact that emerges, however, is the fundamental one that in 1758, this particular bit of land was owned by a Newport merchant, by name Metcalf Bowler. Here in that year he built his house, and that house is the one that still survives, and is known as the Vernon house.

The lot on which it stood was a generous one, extending from Clarke to Spring Streets, a distance of a hundred feet, and for a distance of a hundred and thirty-five feet on Clarke Street. There was thus ample space for the garden, with its usual Newport concomitants of fruit trees, flower borders and vegetables; for the coach house, and, no doubt, slave quarters and offices in the rear.

The house as we see it, probably looks as it did when it was built, though of this we cannot, of course, be sure. The peculiar "rustication" of the outside is an original feature of the Redwood Library, built some ten years earlier by the distinguished English architect, Peter Harrison. This house also has been ascribed to him, though, it seems without sufficient proof, as it lacks the classic effect that marks his style, as shown in the Dudley and Malbone houses, as well as the Redwood Library and town market.

The style which we call "Colonial" and the English "Georgian," was in 1758 practised in all parts of the colonies by builders, whose names are unknown to us, but whose work remains for the admiration of later generations. Worthily did they carry on the traditions of the English school, whose panellings, classic details, and fine carvings so beautified and transformed domestic interiors, during this period. The broad spaces, open vistas and general effect of generous proportion, so characteristic of the style, seemed peculiarly fitted to the spirit of the times, as well as to the medium in which the builders worked. The Vernon house is a typical Colonial mansion, and the builder, whoever he was, was fully equal to his task, and produced a house, comfortable and even distinguished, and fitted to the place it was to hold as the home of a wealthy and dignified merchant of a prosperous town.

One of the most attractive features of the old house, the wide panelled hall, is probably much as Metcalf Bowler saw it. The stairs winding at the back are certainly original, and the arched window above, so typical of the period, adds a most attractive touch. On the second story a like hall runs the length of the house, now however altered by the partitioning off of a room at the front. The north front room on the ground floor is panelled from floor to ceiling. It is not possible to say whether all the interior finish is original. The mantel shelves are undoubtedly later additions, and have been fitted in high or low as circumstances demanded. The south-east room has been remodelled, perhaps immediately after the Revolution.

It is probable that the ceiling beams originally showed—they are now covered by a "furring," perhaps to be attributed to the same date. The old brown stone steps are interesting with their triple approach—the only example of this arrangement in Newport. The original knocker is still on the door.

Such then, comfortable, spacious and dignified, was the home of Metcalf Bowler. Let us inquire as to him, its first proprietor.

It was in the year 1740, that Charles Bowler, an Englishman of substance and position, came to Boston, accompanied by his son, Metcalf, then a boy of fourteen. Buying land on Beacon Hill, he resided there for a time. How his son came to remove to Newport, we do not know. Ten years later, in 1750, we find him here, however, and marrying, in that year, the daughter of Major and Bathsheba Fairchild—Mistress Ann. Doubtless he had already begun that career as a merchant, which was to make him

THE LOWER HALL, VERNON HOUSE

one of the wealthy men of his day. In 1753 Charles Bowler was appointed Collector of Revenues in Newport and followed his son hither, selling most of his property in Boston, and purchasing a fine estate of seventy acres on the island of Rhode Island. Here he resided until his death in 1768, laying out, it may be, the remarkable gardens, which, in his son's time, were so well known.

Metcalf Bowler was thus established, from his earliest manhood, in Newport. These were the days of the town's great and growing prosperity. An important commercial port, it had an extensive trade with the West Indies, Europe and Africa. Numerous as its wharves were, they were continually crowded with vessels, the warehouses which lined them were filled to overflowing, and the streets were thronged with sailors. Merchant-men and whalers discharged their cargoes and refitted, ship building went on in the cove, ropewalks spun the needed cordage, while the raw material brought in was worked up in spermaceti refineries and distilleries. Sugar and molasses were the staples; logwood from Honduras, silks and wines from France, and slaves from Africa were landed on Newport wharves. The slaves brought here were mostly destined for domestic service, as the so-called triangular course of the vessels engaged in the trade—to Africa, the West Indies, and then Newport—drafted off most of these unfortunates to the sugar plantations. There was not at this time the moral objection to the traffic that was felt later, and it is certain that many a Newport fortune was built on this as well as on more respectable foundations.

Newport, then, was a busy port. The opportunities offered here attracted merchants from all parts of the world. There were Huguenots from the Carolinas, Scots who had espoused Prince Charlie's cause, natives of Antigua, Ireland and Germany, as well as Jews from Portugal and the West Indies—perhaps the most enterprising and successful of all. As the town grew in wealth, elegant residences were built, some of which remain to our day, to show the taste and resources of the old Newport merchants. Thames Street in its full length, the Parade and the Point were the favorite residence sections. Built of wood, with gambrel or truss roofs, and often elaborate doorways, the old houses were fine and stately homes, with their true proportions, beautiful panelling and careful and loving treatment of detail. Within were all the luxuries the times afforded—choice china and glass, Turkey carpets, claw-footed mahogany, and Dutch mirrors shining from the dim interiors, not then, as now, universally glorified with white paint. Some panellings were of red cedar, some floor boards, it is said, of mahogany. In the huge old fireplaces blazed great fires of logs; foreign wines and West Indian dainties graced the board, while a retinue of black servants rendered faithful service. Such were the luxuries of a man of wealth in Newport in the middle of the eighteenth century, and doubtless the wealthy ship owner deemed that his lines had fallen to him in pleasant places, as from his western windows he looked out over the blue bay, where his stately vessels would presently come sailing in, bringing him rich cargoes.

So Metcalf Bowler lived. We cannot doubt that he found his home a pleasant one, in its retired yet convenient location. It is recorded that he practised an ample hospitality, and that his style of living was luxurious. He had eleven children, at least one of whom was sent to school in Boston. We owe our knowledge of this to the fact that poor young Penelope died there of the small pox, such a scourge in the eighteenth century. Metcalf Bowler,

UPPER HALL AND STAIRCASE WINDOW, VERNON HOUSE

as a good churchman, was church warden of Trinity. Portraits of him and his wife were painted by Copley, and, it is said, are still in the possession of descendants. A copy of Mrs. Bowler's picture, published in the "Bowler Genealogy," shows her to have been a most attractive woman. Her hair is smoothly drawn back, while her lace cap and the jewels at her throat set off her charm, and the rich satin dress, with falling ruffles of lace, is such as befits a lady of her position. She must have made a fine appearance as she took the air in the family coach—for Metcalf Bowler owned a coach. There was only one other at this time in Newport, the property of Abraham Redwood, principal benefactor of the Redwood Library.

Beside the luxury and busy industry of the time, there was, however, another side to the picture. The eighteenth century was a time of wide-spread unrest. War succeeded war, wherein the good Newport merchants, though reaping profit through their privateers, yet ran great risk of losing their peaceful trading vessels. It was said in 1759 that Newport had lost in the course of trade since the beginning of the Seven Years' War, then in progress, upwards of two millions of money. Metcalf Bowler suffered with others, though, like them, his privateers had brought him in rich prizes. It must have been an exciting time when you never knew whether you would be enriched with "pieces of eight" and ivory, or silks or indigo, brought in by your tall cruisers, or whether a long expected merchant-man would at last be proved a total loss—ship, cargo and all. Newport lost in this way more than a hundred vessels, and it may be questioned whether the colony's sixty privateers went far to make up the great drain on private resources.

A still more serious trouble was in store for Newport—

portents of Revolution, in fact, in the ever growing irritation and annoyance felt in the relations with the Mother Country. The chief trade of the town, as has been said, was with the West Indies. As early as 1733, England had passed what was known as the "Sugar and Molasses Act." This act, passed in the interests of the English islands of the West Indies, imposed a practically prohibitive duty on imports from the French and Spanish colonies. This was ruinous to the interests of a town, founded, as Newport was, on free trade.

For long, the enforcement of the act was not strict in these remote parts of the world. By 1763, however, it was renewed, and its carrying out attempted, in a manner felt to be intolerable by other New England ports, as well as Newport. The measure, as such, was stigmatized as an infringement of the liberty of the subject. The actual enforcement of it here, involving the presence of an armed vessel, to prevent the landing of untaxed goods, was considered most offensive.

The hot bloods of the town involved themselves in skirmishes with King's men, or as our loyal Rhode Islanders termed them, "ministerial tools;" the more farseeing and discreet sought redress in a more regular way. Metcalf Bowler, as one of the latter class, was selected to represent the colony and attend, as commissioner, the convention of the several states, called at New York in October, 1765. This convention met to consider the grievances of the colonies, especially in regard to taxation. Henry Ward, Secretary of the Assembly, was the other delegate. The two gentlemen journeyed together, Metcalf Bowler in his coach, Ward on horseback. The gravity of their mission is indicated by the charge given them by the General Assembly of the colony: " To you, gentlemen, this Assembly have committed concerns of the last consequence to themselves, to their constituents, and to posterity, and we hope that the just sense you entertain of the importance of the trust we have placed in you, will induce you to exert all your capacities to discharge it in such a manner as to do honor to yourselves and service to the colony." The duties of the commission were duly performed. A loyal and dutiful address to his Majesty, King George, was drawn up, and declarations of opinion respecting the rights and liberties of the colonists were added to it. These were forwarded to Great Britain, and may have had a share in the repeal of the hated Stamp Act in the following March. The commissioners were thanked for their services and styled "faithful and judicious."

The Stamp Act was repealed March 18th, 1766. On the anniversary of that repeal, March 18th, 1767, there was great rejoicing in Newport. Salvoes were fired, thirteen lanterns for the thirteen colonies were hung on the Liberty Tree at the head of Thames Street, and in the evening, " Hon. Metcalf Bowler gave an elegant entertainment to a number of gentlemen, true friends of Liberty," thus again proving himself of the number of those who were heart and soul for American freedom. This was the more praiseworthy in Metcalf Bowler, that many men, born, like him, in England, chose rather to espouse the cause of the King as against the rebel colonies. Newport had perhaps an unusual number of these "Tories," as they were called; salaried officials or simply merchants, who consistently worked against the cause so dear to all true patriots, choosing rather to throw in their lot with the constituted authority.

In the following year Metcalf Bowler was made one of

a committee to prepare an address to King George, which, setting forth the colonies' grievances, requests the royal interposition in behalf of violated rights, for—"Your Majesty (is) ever mindful of the welfare and happiness of all your subjects, however remote." Thus loyal to the King was Rhode Island in 1768, ascribing all its troubles to his false advisers and ministers. In this year, Charles Bowler died and Metcalf Bowler, as eldest son, inherited, by English law, his father's property. The country place now came into his hands.

This estate, situated just north of Vaucluse, on the east shore of the island, was famous in its day. The house is still standing, though now in an advanced state of decay, and shows a fine doorway, suggesting the work of Munday, the builder of the Colony house. The front of the house consisted of one large room, with the door opening directly into it, making a banqueting hall of generous proportions, a unique arrangement for Rhode Island.

Traces still remain of stone barns, sheds and greenhouse wall, and the offices of the place were evidently on a large scale. The pleasure gardens, said to have covered eleven acres, have vanished, save for a few hardy flowers run wild. Their fame has come down to us, however, as the most splendid and best cultivated on the island. The formal planting was considered remarkable, with its fountains and fish pools. It is a pity that nothing remains to us of all this elaborate garden, not even the box, which at Vaucluse has grown to so remarkable a size, or the cedars, as at Malbone's gardens. The greenhouses were considered very fine, and here it was, says that amusing chronicler of the olden time, Thomas R. Hazard, that the first Rhode Island greening originated.

Growing in a porcelain tub, presented by a Persian prince, it was brought home by one of Metcalf Bowler's captains from the site of ancient Eden,--surely a princely gift to the good people of Newport!

A perhaps better authenticated fact of this fine country place is that the gate posts were graced, English fashion, by a couple of heraldic eagles, gilded. Charles Bowler's coat-of-arms, still extant, shows an eagle as its crest. These eagles, carved in wood, met with various vicissitudes, after Metcalf Bowler's time, one of them serving as sign to the Eagle Tavern, later the United States Hotel. They finally came to rest at the second story level of two Thames Street business houses, one of them Mr. Hammett's old bookstore, later Mr. Hart's. Children used to be told that these two old eagles came down at twelve o'clock to get their dinners and, I suppose, could never disprove it, owing to the fact that they, too, were dining at that hour.

This estate, so finely laid out and cultivated, was considered one of the sights of the Island, and strangers were taken to see it. Dr. Stiles, the Congregational minister and diarist, tells of riding out to visit it in 1770. Unfortunately he gives no account of it, reporting, instead, a metaphysical argument with a brother divine on the way there and back.

In the same year, 1768, Metcalf Bowler, now for the first time returned as deputy from Portsmouth instead of, as in the past four years, Newport, was made speaker of the General Assembly, an honor which he was to retain for nineteen years. Whether he, from this time, resided at his country place or not, he retained his town house for five years more, disposing of it finally in 1773.

His political activities still continued. In 1774, he read

at the great meeting at Fanueil Hall, in Boston, Rhode Island's circular letter, inviting a "firm and close union" between the colonies. The times of trouble now drawing near, he was made a member of the "Committee of Safety" and appointed one of those commissioned to procure arms for the defense of the colony. In 1776 he was made Chief Justice of the Supreme Court.

The third year of the Revolution saw Metcalf Bowler removed to Providence, where he passed the remainder of his life, though he still retained his country place until 1786. He appears to have been much reduced in fortune at the close of the great National struggle, the times having ruined him, as they did many another man. Highly respected in his new home, church warden of St. John's, he died in 1789, no longer the wealthy merchant, but untroubled by his changed fortunes, and honored by all his associates. His connection with the old house carries with it only worthy and dignified memories.

As has been said, Metcalf Bowler's connection with the house terminated in 1773. In this year he sold it to another Newport merchant and ship owner, William Vernon. It thus became the "Vernon House," a name it seems likely always to retain. As the story of Metcalf Bowler is largely bound up with the commercial prosperity of the town, so William Vernon stands for us as a type of those self-sacrificing patriots, whose lot it was to aid the course of the young republic, in the time of sore stress now close at hand.

The old house is now to pass through strange scenes—war and famine are to harass Newport town, and the tread of an invader to be heard in her streets.

The Vernons were of old Rhode Island stock. The first of the family, Daniel Vernon, came to Newport from

CORNER CUPBOARD IN THE DINING-ROOM, VERNON HOUSE
Vernon Chairs, Table and Silver.
On the Floor, Continental Currency found in the Vernon House

England in 1666. Though he spent most of his life in Narragansett, from his time those who bore the name were closely identified with Newport. In 1773, the Vernons to be found here were typical men of their day, in position, wealth and enterprise. The representatives of the family at this time were three brothers, Samuel, Thomas and William—all men of mark.

Thomas Vernon, the second brother, was royal postmaster in Newport, a position he had held for almost thirty years. He was also senior warden of Trinity Church, and Secretary of the Redwood Library. His house stood on the west side of Division Street. Unfortunately for him, he espoused the cause of the King, when the breach came, and became a most unpopular man, being sent away in 1776 into an unpleasant sort of exile among the towns of the upper part of the state. Party feeling ran high in those days, and Whigs and Tories were well-nigh at one another's throats in Newport.

The other two brothers, unlike Thomas, were ardent supporters of the cause of liberty. These two constituted together the famous firm of S. and W. Vernon, merchants and ship owners, whose ventures were sent out far and wide, to Europe, the West Indies and Africa. Samuel, the oldest, lived in the house just west of the Thayer School on Church Street, later called the Olyphant house, a fine and substantial mansion. William Vernon, the youngest, is of special interest to us, for he it was who purchased the house in which we are interested. Born in 1719 he was fifty-four years of age at this time. His wife, Judith Harwood, was, curiously enough, a direct descendant of Jeremy Clarke. She, however, had died more than ten years earlier. An older sister, Mistress Esther Vernon, presided over the establishment, and two boys, Samuel and William, sixteen and fourteen years of age, completed the family. The contrast must have been marked in the life of the old house. In Metcalf Bowler's day, the crowd of children, with the sweet matron at their head; now, the elderly spinster, and the well-grown boys, doubtless serious with the premature manliness of the day. One can imagine them saluting their honored father as they met at the morning meal in the sunny, pleasant dining room.

We do not know where William Vernon had lived previous to his purchase of the Vernon House. It may well be that he had long admired his brother merchant's fine house, and when the opportunity came, despite the doubtful times, thought it worth his while to secure so comfortable and dignified a home. He paid two thousand pounds, old tenor, for house, garden and appurtenances.

Here, then, did William Vernon set up his household gods, furnishing the finely proportioned square rooms with the elegant mahogany furniture of the period with its carving and claw feet. The heavy, handsome old chairs, highboys, gilt mirrors and other fine pieces are still recalled as forming part of the old-time aspect of the house. A sedan chair is still preserved, which was probably a part of William Vernon's plenishing, though it may have been brought from France by his son twenty years later. It is the only one we know of in Newport, and is quite likely to have been used by the worthy merchant himself, as men were not infrequently carried in these convenient small affairs. Black and shiny without, lined with cream colored broadcloth within, it recalls to us Colonial days, ball, revel and assembly, as well as the muddy streets of olden times, and fine clothes which needed protection. We are fortunate in the possession of this interesting old

OLD SEDAN CHAIR BELONGING TO THE VERNON FAMILY

relic, which is now to be preserved in the Vernon house, having been presented by Mrs. Hodson, the daughter of Mr. Read, a later owner.

To return to the house—we know that there were paper hangings on the walls and that the hearths were of marble. Carpets "even on the stairs" were common articles of luxury soon after this time, and may have graced the Vernon house. Handsome and plentiful silver decked the sideboard, and tall silver candlesticks lighted the domestic interior, while slaves, both men and women, waited on Master, Mistress and the two young gentlemen. A portion of William Vernon's fine service of Crown Derby is still preserved, and is in the possession of his descendants.

It seems a pity that William Vernon was not left longer in peaceful possession of his new home. The war clouds, however, were already gathering over New England, and Newport, sensitive as a commercial port must be, felt the growing tension of the relations between the colonies and the old country. That daring act, the scuttling of the sloop Liberty, had already taken place in Newport harbor, and the commissioners on the affair of the "Gaspee" schooner were even now sitting in Newport, charged with the duty of ferretting out the perpetrators of that bold deed of destruction. If found, they were to be indicted for high treason, a consummation, however, never attained; as, though doubtless everyone in Providence knew them, reliable evidence was impossible to secure. The worthy chief justices of the commission were therefore compelled reluctantly to return to their homes, vowing that this people "would require a gentleman of very extraordinary qualifications to model them into due subordination and decorum."

Following, came a more serious menace—the "Rose"

frigate—Captain Wallace, Commander—to enforce with severity the revenue laws, and to harass, as far as might be, these rebels, who had so far forgotten their duty to his most gracious majesty, King George the Third. This was in 1774. The task assigned him seems to have been a congenial one to the harsh captain. His high handed proceedings, we cannot doubt, caused a helpless wrath at Newport, which fanned the flame of disaffection to white heat. The firm of S. and W. Vernon was among those who suffered from Wallace's methods. Their Jamaica brig, the "Royal Charlotte," seized in Newport harbor, was taken to Boston, and there confiscated with her cargo. It is probable that the Vernons, as conspicuous friends of Liberty, were singled out for persecution, by way of discouraging others of their way of thinking.

Times must have looked dark indeed to the merchants of Newport. An all-but declared enemy was at their door, their commerce cut off, their ships, returning unawares, captured. With the news of Lexington and Concord, a break with the mother country was seen to be inevitable. Newport firms were urged by their correspondents to get their vessels out of New England with all speed. It was felt by all merchants here that not only was their business at an end, but—when hostilities should break out—that Newport was a most probable objective point for "ministerial" vessels. As a matter of fact, the "Rose" frigate had by June, 1775, been joined by a number of other vessels, making a fleet of twelve, great and small. Twice did Wallace threaten to bombard the town, unless provided with "beef and beer." The second time, the danger seemed so pressing that the streets were crowded with carts and chaises, filled with people making the best of their way away from the point of danger.

Prudent Newport heads of families had ere this made up their minds that the "once happy town" was now no place for them. By October, it was calculated that three-fourths of the inhabitants had departed. Houses were left with only one or two to care for them, shops were closed; the Tories, of course, had no objection to remaining, as things were going very much to their mind; others took steps to remove their families, and, so far as might be, their valuables, to places of greater safety.

William Vernon, however, for the time, remained in Newport. In the midst of the "consternation and distress" prevailing, he afforded what aid he could, assisting in October in the removal of the poor of the town from this most exposed position to other places.

Early in 1776, Newport patriots were much cheered by the departure of Wallace's fleet. They immediately set about constructing defenses and securing cannon for the protection of the town. All allegiance to Great Britain was thrown off by the State in May. On the eighteenth of July, the Declaration of Independence was read at the State House, while thirteen guns were fired at Fort Liberty—no longer Fort George, and our Colonial brigade, drawn up on the Parade, fired thirteen salvoes of musketry. This exultation, however, was short-lived. By November, most of the cannon had been removed to protect the upper reaches of the bay, so pressing seemed the danger of invasion, and it was seen to be impossible, should the enemy elect to go into winter quarters in Newport, to prevent such action.

William Vernon now felt that he could remain no longer. His son, William, was at Princeton, pursuing his studies, so there were only his sister and eldest son, Samuel, to be considered. Aunt Esther possibly had Tory proclivities—

or, it may be, simply disliked leaving her home—in any case she obstinately refused to go. It was arranged that Samuel should remain to watch over the Vernon property and affairs. The silver was buried, but the household furniture in great part, left in position. William Vernon himself only awaited the actual arrival of the British fleet to depart.

On the 7th of December they were descried—81 sail, under Sir Peter Parker, 11 men-of-war, and 70 transports. It was now incumbent on a prominent patriot like Vernon to be gone. All possibility of serving his country while remaining in Newport was at an end. Accordingly on the morning of the 8th, he, with many others, departed, leaving the town and island. On the same day he wrote back to his son from Swansea, on his way to Rehoboth, where "Sister Sanford" was now settled, addressing him as—

"Dear Sammy:—

"I am full of anxiety for you and your Aunt, yet I am full of hope that no real ill will happen to anybody at Newport. I mean as to bodily injury. Yet to be amongst enemies is disagreeable and such a feeling that I should not choose, and should be glad and rejoice if every part of my family was with me." "I hope and pray a kind Providence will protect us and direct you in whatever design you propose, not doubting you will conduct with caution and prudence. Don't, my dear son, be intimidated or hurried into any mad and hasty measure. Endeavor to comfort your Aunt, whose obstinacy prevented her from going up to Sister Sanford's. Adieu, my son."

Writing to his son William on the occasion, he tells him that he brought off with him the three negroes, Barre, Accran and Ceasar, leaving behind Cadys, Belinda and her child; and that Aunt Esther, whom "I could not prevail with to leave Newport," had (perhaps with some qualms now that the English were really arrived), removed herself and the negroes to "your Uncle Tom's." Thomas Vernon, now returned from his unwilling exile as a Tory, was no doubt happy to receive his sister in his Division Street house, and to afford her any protection she might require.

. William Ellery, the Signer, a particular friend of William Vernon's, writes to him soon after, "I wonder that you should hesitate about my approbation of your flight. It would have been worse than death to you to have been exposed to the insolence of the Tories. They would have triumphed * * * at your captivity."

The much-dreaded enemy, who now invaded Newport under the royal standard of King George, consisted of forces, divided nearly equally into English and Hessians, 6500 troops in all. Sir Henry Clinton was in command. Most of them landed somewhat higher on the island, but ere William Vernon had been gone many hours, boat loads of soldiers were disembarking at Long Wharf, and the gleam of the red coats was seen on the Parade—O, sad day for Newport! The Tories were in their glory, welcoming those whom they considered friends, and pointing out the houses of prominent patriots. We cannot doubt that William Vernon's house was one of these; but it is probable that Brother Thomas would keep watch over the property, as well as over the person of his young nephew, as he seems to have been on affectionate terms with William, in spite of their differences of opinion. The Vernon counting house, it is known, was ransacked and all the papers tumbled out, but this may very probably have occurred later.

It was now a question of securing quarters for the troops.

The officers were bestowed in the most comfortable loyalists' houses, the soldiers quartered in those, often vacant, belonging to friends of Liberty. What a change for the staid old town! So large a body of men must have been difficult to place at such short notice, and the King's uniform and Hessian green coat, now thronging the streets, doubtless meant discomfort and misery for many a humble citizen.

It would seem that Samuel Vernon did not remain long in Newport. In April, one of the Rehoboth family speaks of "Cousin Sam" as with them. He adds "We hear that Aunt Esther is heartily tired of that once pleasant and agreeable place: (Newport). We don't learn anything particular about your house or servants. About a hundred and fifty buildings have been pulled down, we hear, for fuel."

Newport had, indeed, ceased to be an agreeable place of residence. War times necessarily wrought havoc with its even, comfortable way of life. Churches were turned into riding schools, the Court House to a hospital, trees were destroyed for fire wood, the cheaper class of buildings torn down for the same purpose. The guttural speech of the Auspachers was heard on every hand; the swagger of the British red-coat proclaimed that he felt at home in this old town, his by right of war. No longer did the aristocratic, luxurious merchant pace on his homeward way, but groups of careless soldiers swung down the hill streets, horses clattered over the stones and the most exclusive portals received, perforce, guests, arrogant, and little disposed to courtesy.

The town was destined to endure three years of foreign occupation. It is wonderful that more harm was not done in the closely built part of the town. Earl Percy, who commanded at first for six months, was a kindly man, and would discourage vandalism. It is said that, on finding that books were being stolen from the Redwood Library, he stationed a soldier at the door, to prevent such despoliation. His successor, the hated Prescott, held sway for over two years. Of an overbearing and bullying nature, disliked even by his own people, he earned for himself an unenviable reputation. The Quakers doffed the hat to no man, and this failure to do him honor particularly enraged the General. His only recourse, when so ignored, was to knock the offending broad brim off with his cane. The streets became less safe after nightfall during his rule and the Hessians were allowed more license. When General Prescott was captured by "bold Barton," the town went wild with joy. Crape was affixed to Loyalist doors, occasioning much sly mirth, and saucy boys walked about with handkerchiefs in their hands, pretending to weep when any Tory appeared, as overcome with grief for this sad visitation.

The Loyalists, as was natural, found a measure of dubious joy in the presence of the alien. Young people danced, though their country was in such sore distress, and the Tory belles made a deep impression on the younger set among the English officers. And so, perhaps echoing for the last time the toasts of Englishmen to King George, certainly looking out on a coming and going of private and officer, red coat and sabre and bearskin cap, the old house wore out the three years of war.

Meanwhile, how fared William Vernon? Very busy was he with activities, designed to make uncomfortable the town's uninvited guests, as well as other Britons engaged in the war. Before his departure from Newport, he had been sounded by William Ellery, then newly a member of the Marine Committee of Congress, as to his willingness to form part of a Navy Board for the Eastern Department. The Marine Committee sorely felt their lack of maritime knowledge and experience, and William Vernon, as a practical man, and large ship owner, was peculiarly fit for so important a position. In May, 1777, such a board was created, with three members, James Warren, of Massachusetts, John Deshon, of Connecticut, and William Vernon, of Rhode Island. William Vernon was from the first, and as long as the Navy Board lasted, its president.

The duties before the newly-formed board were numerous and pressing. The need of a really efficient navy was extreme. The ever-menacing British ships presented a most serious obstacle to success in arms along our extended seaboard. There were a few vessels already in the possession of the United Colonies, and the thirteen frigates authorized by Congress were building. The various colonies also were maintaining small navies of their own, these of course not being under the jurisdiction of the Federal authority. Commodore Esek Hopkins was still in command of the fleet. Privateers supplemented the Continental and State service, and incidentally by their superior attractions made the manning of the more regular vessels most difficult. Opposed to these were more than a hundred British vessels, many of them superior to anything the Americans could show.

The instructions given to the Navy Board, or "Board of Assistants to the Marine Committee" were dated July 10, 1777. Its members are to superintend all naval and marine affairs in the four Eastern States, to regulate the building and fitting out of ships for the United Colonies, to collect and provide material and stores for the same, and to keep a register of all such vessels, with their officers and men—surely arduous duties for three men to perform, even practical and experienced ones.

William Vernon now removed to Boston, where, from this time, he gave his valuable services to the nation until the abolition of the Navy Board in 1781, little more than a year prior to the signing of provisional articles of peace. During these four years, his knowledge of marine affairs, ability and devotion to the cause were of great value. Laboring under great discouragements, suffering from a shortage of money, delays of all kinds, disappointments in the manning of vessels, inability to get the ships to sea owing to the blockading British and many other difficulties, the Navy Board had a most trying post to fill. Courts-martial, too, were a part of their duty, of officers whose ships had been lost to the powerful foe. The services of this board have hardly been appreciated as they deserve, and William Vernon's principal claim to the gratitude of posterity undoubtedly rests on his skilful management of the naval affairs which came under his control. Amid many reverses, our small Navy accomplished a surprising amount, and it has been well said, "The Revolution must have failed but for its sailors." Harassing the enemy, holding open communication with France, bringing in invaluable contributions of stores and munitions of war captured from time to time, the ships which William Vernon superintended gave a good account of themselves and while, one by one, they fell a melancholy prey to a vastly superior enemy, yet they played their part, and an important one, in the great struggle for American independence. Beside giving his services, William Vernon, it is said, advanced large sums to the government in its time of need, which were only in part repaid. His losses in the way of trade were also considerable, yet seem not to have distressed him. In a letter to a friend he says "Mammon is no idol of mine. If we establish our rights and liberties upon a firm and lasting basis, in the winding up of this bloody contest, I am content; although I own if I could come at the property our enemies are possessed of belonging to me, it would increase the pleasure. I do assure you it is no less a sum than twelve thousand pounds sterling, at least, beside my real estate in Newport, yet I can with truth say, it never broke my rest a moment."

Samuel Vernon 2nd seems to have joined his father in Boston, and engaged in business there. Quite different and more romantic was the career of his younger brother. He had been sent to Princeton to complete his studies, where in 1776 at a "somewhat hurried commencement," he was graduated and delivered an oration on "Standing Armies." It was planned that he pursue some postgraduate studies, but imminent danger of attack from the British led to his "precipitate flight" from Princeton in December, 1776, his father not knowing of his whereabouts for six months. Mr. Ellery, always interested in his friend's affairs, says, under date of February, 1777: "I lament that your son hath been drove from his studies, for he is an agreeable, promising youth and bids fair to be serviceable to mankind." Early in the following year William Vernon determined to send young William abroad, as he says, "with a view to accomplish him for business, either as a merchant or in any other way that he might be most useful in future to his country and our rising independent states."

The honorable John Adams had at this time been appointed Commissioner to France and Mr. Vernon resolved to intrust his son to his care. "As he is young, just out of the University, his genius and talents not formed or scarcely known, I left it with Mr. Adams to fix him for three or four years in a situation most agreeable and best adapted to his disposition and abilities."

John Adams was sailing on the "Boston" frigate, with his son, John Quincy Adams, then eleven years of age, and accordingly on his departure, February 15th, 1778, young William Vernon set out on his travels. William Ellery writes on the occasion, "The Boston hath on board a pretious cargo. May she carry it safe to France." The voyage was tempestuous, the frigate was chased by the enemy and "the captain of the mainmast was struck with the lightning," yet in spite of all, the Boston arrived safely in Bordeaux, April 1st, a short journey for those days. Here Mr. Adams established his young charge, and left him in a position to acquire the French language and the rudiments of business, with a merchant of that town. Frequent reports came to Mr. Vernon of his son's diligence and hopeful parts.

In March, 1778, the small pox was raging in Boston, and as William Vernon had never had the disease, he removed to Providence and directed the motions of the Navy Board from that point. In October the sickness slackened sufficiently to allow him to return, much to the satisfaction of his associates. Soon after this, Samuel, his son, returned to Newport, perhaps to watch over the property there; and probably from this time was much back and forth. While in Newport he must have shared in the hopes and fears of his townsmen there, in the times of scarcity and the rigors of the great "Hessian Storm."

The time of investment was now drawing to a close. Change of campaign by the British commanders led to a decision to evacuate Newport. That which the combined French and Americans had not been able to effect, was now to come to pass. On the 11th of October, 1779, the orders were issued; on the 12th, the transport arrived, and on the 25th, the exodus actually took place. All royalists, who desired to do so, were allowed to accompany the fleet, taking with them their effects. It is said that 56, with their families, availed themselves of the permission. Among them was the Tory sheriff, Walter Chaloner, to whom we owe a grudge, for he it was who carried off our records. These, suffering shipwreck on the way, were seriously injured and in part lost.

What a day was that for the town that saw the invaders depart! All day long the troops marched through the streets, embarking at Brenton's Point, near what is now Fort Adams, in small boats. Orders had been given that all the inhabitants were to remain within doors. "Newport looked as if everybody was dead," we are told. "The doors and windows were shut, not a soul to be seen, and this was done to guard against desertion." At ten o'clock at night, the fleet, one hundred and ten sail, convoyed by three men-of-war, sailed out of the harbor.

Newport had now before her the task of rehabilitation, and long and slow it proved. With her commerce destroyed, her merchants established elsewhere, more than five hundred houses destroyed and an estimated damage of £124,000, it may easily be imagined that the once prosperous town found itself in an exhausted and prostrate condition. Most of the wealthy Tory families were gone, the enterprising Hebrew merchants as well, and other towns profited by what Newport lost.

With the new year, however, came hopes of a pleasanter chapter in the old town's fortunes. America's steady friend, Lafayette, had secured from the King of France the promise of an expeditionary corps, and in May it was rumored that the French allies were to be stationed at Newport. This rumor was confirmed, and on July 11th, 1780, the fleet arrived. This fleet was direct from Brest, and consisted of twelve men-of-war and thirty-two transports, carrying a force of over 5000 men. The Admiral was "His Excellency, Monsieur le Chevalier de Ternay," and the Commander-in-Chief, "His Excellency, Monsieur le Comte de Rochambeau"—Jean-Baptiste-Donatien de Vimeur, Count de Rochambeau, to give him his full name.

At noon the French general landed, and we may suppose that preparations were at once begun for receiving the officers and men of the allied forces. The allies were most welcome, for what they brought and for what they promised, yet Rochambeau tells us that nobody appeared in the streets and those who looked from the windows seemed sad and depressed. He spoke to the principal inhabitants and told them that more forces were to follow, and that the King of France was prepared to support them with all his power. Perhaps poor, war-worn Newport found it hard to believe that any good thing could come to her, and that these were friends, able, and willing to help. Once convinced, however, the townsmen felt that something must be done to signalize so auspicious an occasion, and, accordingly, the town council met at once and voted an illumination for the following night, to celebrate the arrival of "the fleet and army of his most Christian Majesty, the illustrious ally of the States, now within the harbor and town of Newport." An illumination in those days consisted of lighted houses, and therefore it was voted that a box of candles should be provided, for the benefit of those who could not afford to buy them for themselves. The resolution of the Town Council was forthwith published by beat of drum.

Meanwhile General Heath was hastening down the bay, bringing Washington's greetings to the allies. Owing to an inopportune calm, he did not reach Newport until midnight. Early next morning he waited on the Count de Rochambeau, and with him on Admiral de Ternay, on board his flagship. With General Heath, came Major Lyman, one of his official family, who spoke French well, and it is said, was the first American to board the French ships. Many of the French officers were unacquainted with English, and an interpreter must have often been needed.

At ten o'clock of the twelfth of July, the Admiral saluted the town with thirteen guns, which was returned with a like number. The landing of the troops was now at once begun, as there were many sick, foi whom it was desirable to find comfortable quarters. Scurvy was a great plague in the long sea voyages of the day, and it was seventy days since the fleet had left Brest. That evening the illumination took place. The principal streets had been ordered lighted. These were "Thames Street, Congress, (heretofore called Queen Street,) Lewis Street (heretofore called King Street,) Broad Street, the street leading over the Point bridge, and the street leading from the Long Wharf to the Point battery." These, in modern parlance are--Thames Street, Washington Square, Franklin Street, Broadway, Farewell Street and Washington Street. No doubt the effect was fine. The diarist, Dr. Stiles, tells us that "the Whigs put thirteen Lights in the Windows, the Tories or doubtfuls four or six. The Quakers did not chuse their Lights should shine before men, and their Windows were broken." The illumination was kept up until ten o'clock, and in addition thirteen "grand rockets" were fired from in front of the State House. A letter of the time speaks of the brilliant appearance of the French officers then on shore, and of the joyful feelings of every friend of Liberty on this happy occasion. General Heath says that the reception accorded them gave "great pleasure and satisfaction" to the allies.

The landing of the troops now was proceeded with. It took four days to bring the sick ashore. Four hundred of them were placed in the improvised hospitals at Newport— the State House, Dr. Hopkins' meeting house and various private houses in the town. The remaining sick, six or seven hundred in number, were taken to Providence or elsewhere. The troops were encamped to the south of Newport and near the cliffs.

It was now necessary to find suitable quarters for the officers. The best houses in town were selected—Governor Wanton's, on Thames Street, Captain Maudsley's at the head of Franklin Street, Colonel Wanton's on the Point, Colonel Malbone's on Thames Street. To the Commander-in-Chief was assigned the Vernon House—surely an honor for the old mansion, and an indication that it was regarded as as comfortable and commodious a dwelling as any in town. Here then, Rochambeau established himself. Tradition points to the north parlor as the one used as his office, and where his desk stood. This seems probable, as it is more retired in situation than the rooms *en suite* on the other side of the hall.

With the Count came his son, Donatien-Marie-Joseph de Vimeur, Vicomte de Rochambeau. He bore the rank of Colonel in the regiment de Bourbonnais, and also acted as aide to his father. Rochambeau's other aides were the

Count de Fersen, the Marquis de Damas, the Baron de Closen, Count Mathieu Dumas and Rochambeau's nephew, Dupont de Lauberdière. A brilliant band of youthful nobles was thus gathered. All but the Vicomte de Rochambeau were domiciled, not in the old house, but near at hand, either just across the street on "New Lane" or on Spring Street.

As headquarters of the general, the Vernon house now became the center of great activities. Councils of war were held, officers came and went ; deep were the consultations and important the decisions arrived at in the north parlor. It is no light matter to be commander-in-chief of six thousand men, who are in a strange country without occupation. The remarkable record of the French soldiers in Newport shows how well drilled and how well intentioned they were. Not a pig or chicken was commandeered, not an apple touched from the laden trees close to their lines, or an ear of corn taken from the corn fields. An interchange of courtesies characterized the intercourse between the American militiamen and the foreign soldiers, each of whom found much to admire in the other. Six days after the arrival of the French, William Vernon despatched his son, Samuel, then in Boston, with a letter of greeting to Admiral de Ternay, saying "the bearer, Mr. Vernon's son, will be happy in having it in his power of rendering Mr. de Ternay or any of his connection every service possible." Whether the tender of the Vernon house was among these services we are not informed.

The new tenant of the mansion was in every way a most distinguished man. At this time fifty years of age, he had been governor of Vendome and of Villefranche, brigadier-general in the French campaigns, and recipient of the grand cross of St. Louis. An experienced soldier and a

NORTH PARLOR, Traditionally Rochambeau's Office

man of solid worth, he was Lafayette's choice for the difficult position of commander-in-chief. In person rather small, keen of glance, dignified in manner, he combined concentration of purpose with an easy and courteous bearing, and conciliated all parties. He never hesitated to subordinate his own interests to the great object he had in view, and held back with a firm hand the hasty and impetuous young officers under his command. His character has been compared to that of Washington. Fortitude, endurance and equanimity were its leading points. Indifferent to criticism or blame, he took what he considered the wisest path, giving to the nation the ripe judgment of an experienced soldier, and to his own forces the example of a wise, restrained and unmoved leader. America owes much to him, as is universally recognized, and he is undoubtedly the most distinguished guest, bar one, that the old house has received within its walls.

We may now imagine Rochambeau sitting at his desk in the north room, deep in the despatches whereby he kept in touch with his general, Washington, or stepping from the door, prepared for the receiving of his troops or supervision of the camps. Tradition says that, when on horseback, he carried a large black muff, (a mark of dignity,) and that when he rode, a running footman scoured before him, dressed all in white and with plumes in his cap. The young officers who frequented the house were also birds of gay plumage. In their green coats with white facings, tight red breeches and high boots, silver epaulets, and chapeaux edged with white and sporting the tri-colored cockade, they must have presented a brilliant appearance. No wonder the hearts of the Newport maidens were fluttered by so much splendor, combined as it was with rank, youth and high spirits.

On hearing of Rochambeau's arrival, Washington at once despatched Lafayette to greet his friends and the country's allies. The young and gallant Marquis arrived on the 20th, nine days after the landing and proceeded to headquarters, thus adding one more to the distinguished visitors to the Vernon house.

On the following day there was great excitement in Newport, at the news of the British fleet seen in the offing. The danger was real, as the soldiers were in poor condition for an attack, and the defenses were not yet fully completed. The fleet continued to cruise about for several days, but did not dare to attack the French in their strong position. M. Blanchard, commissary-general and diarist, dined with Rochambeau on the 22nd at his quarters, and reports that the general publicly said that he wished the English would attempt it. M. Blanchard remarks that it was as well, under the circumstances, that no attack was made, but adds, "M. de Rochambeau did well to appear secure." "At this dinner were several Americans, all good patriots, and an English officer, who was a prisoner. They addressed some sharp words to each other"—as was not surprising with their very divergent views on the subject of that menacing fleet.

As a matter of fact, Newport had, as narrowly as possible, escaped a second investiture by the English. It had been planned to intercept the French and reach the harbor ahead of them, and only the steadiness of the admiral in keeping his course across the ocean, and refusing tempting offers of battle made to him, had prevented it.

The day of St. Louis was the next interesting event in Newport. This was the "*jour de l'an*" of the King, and loyalty demanded a celebration from the French officers.

The ships were accordingly decorated, salutes were fired, and we cannot doubt that a banquet closed the joyful day, at which his Majesty was toasted with generous bumpers. This was on August 25th. On the 29th, a party of guests, of a sort most interesting to the strangers, was received in Newport. This was a band of Indian chiefs—Iroquois, from Canada and Northern New York. Their allegiance was supposed to be wavering toward the English, and it was deemed a stroke of policy to invite them to witness the good understanding between the French and the Americans. These children of the forest created a great impression on the Frenchmen, who record the painted faces, the gashed ears and scanty clothing of the savages: "They complimented M. de Rochambeau, who received them very kindly, and gave them some presents, among other things some red blankets," which had been bought at Brest at the moment of departure. Each chief was also given a medal with King Louis's coronation scene thereon. "They dined that night with him at his quarters. I saw them at table for an instant," says the diarist, Blanchard. "They behaved themselves well there, and ate cleanly enough." It must have been a curious sight—the courtly French general in his uniform of green and silver, feasting the blanketed savages on sumptuous viands, the like of which they had never seen, and attending to their service at the hands of his numerous retinue of servants. The Indians witnessed a review of the French troops, and themselves entertained their hosts with a war dance, "uttering harsh and disagreeable cries" and reminding the Frenchmen of the movements of their own peasants in treading out the wine. After four days they departed, expressing themselves as highly gratified by their entertainment.

On the first of October, the French minister plenipotentiary, le Chevalier de la Luzerne, came from Philadelphia to confer with Rochambeau, and was received with great ceremony. It was agreed to send a minister to France to ask for reinforcements, in view of the superior naval force of the British, which kept the French inactive in Newport. The younger Rochambeau was sent on this important mission. Taking advantage of a severe storm, the "Amazone" frigate slipped out through the blockading English, and reached France in safety. The Vicomte successfully performed his task, returning in the following April, with a large amount of money, and the promise of a fleet—this last afterwards made good with most important consequences.

While the Chevalier de la Luzerne was here another visitor was received—Dr. Ezra Stiles, sometime pastor of the Congregational Church in Newport and now President of Yale College. He dined on the 7th of October "at the General's—de Rochambeau, in a splendid manner. There were perhaps 30 at table. I conversed with the General in Latin. He speaks it tolerably." This report would seem to indicate that Rochambeau was not especially conversant with the English language. Latin was often used in communication with the allies when a common language failed.

Rochambeau now felt the need of a meeting place for his officers. They chafed under the enforced inaction, and it is probable that he thought that an assembly hall where they might entertain their friends and one another, would serve as an outlet for youthful spirits. In addition, the Vernon house was limited in its accommodation. It is difficult to conceive of thirty sitting down to dinner in the south-east room, then, as always, the dining room. The new hall could be used for banquets as well as for dances. Towards the end of November, accordingly, there was built in the garden to the north of the house, what was long known as the "French Hall." This hall, traditionally square and known to have been 26 feet on one measure, may have been altered over into the stable which later stood on this site. At the extreme north-west corner of the lot, with a door opening to the south towards the Vernon house, this little structure was square and resembled the old house in general style, though without the rustication. It may well have been the "French Hall" adapted to later needs. It was certainly not the old coach house, as it had no place for carriages.

William Vernon, writing to his son, Samuel, then at Newport, under date of December 5th, 1781, says, "I understand Gen. Rochambeau had not your leave for building an assembly room in the garden. I can't think it was polite of him." General Rochambeau, however, while in Boston on the eighteenth of the same month, called to pay his respects to Mr. Vernon, quite possibly with the intention of explaining his action.

The hall was completed in the new year, and "began to be frequented," says Blanchard, "early in January." During this month and February, we hear of "elegant balls" given to the ladies of Newport by the Count de Deuxponts, and the handsome brothers Viomenil, baron and viscount. We can imagine the scene—the newly-built assembly room, lighted by candles in sconces, and surely, in January, warmed by a blazing fire, the uniformed musicians, the discreet dowagers, and, observed of all observers, the brilliant band of young noblemen in their gala attire of white broadcloth, turned back with pink, blue or green according to their corps. In minuet or contra dance, they lead out the gay young Newport beauties, whose charms they so admire. Perhaps it was after some such entertainment that a diamond ring scratched on the panes of the old Vernon house the names of the lovely Misses Hunter, interwoven with love-knots and Cupid's arrows—inscriptions, now, alas! disappeared. The ladies of the day must also have presented an attractive appearance in their lutestrings and brocades, their raised headdresses decked with the French gauzes which Chastellux (one of the French officers) was so surprised to find " in the wilds of America."

Washington's birthday was this year celebrated for the first time of which we have knowledge. King Louis' feast day had been honored by the General at his camp, and the French now reciprocated. Rochambeau writes to Washington of " the effusion and gladness of our hearts " on the occasion. The celebration took place on February 12th, as the 11th was Sunday, and the old style was still in use.

The winter thus passed away quietly and without any change in the situation. Destouches, now in command of the naval forces, sent out a portion of his squadron, a ship of the line and two frigates, for a dash against the enemy in Chesapeake Bay. They returned March 30th, after a successful raid, and Destouches then proposed sending out the rest of his fleet for further attack; carrying with him a part of the land forces. This was a very important move, and one Washington had much at heart. On Rochambeau communicating the new plans to him, the General seems to have somewhat hastily decided to come to Newport, see what was being done and have an interview again face to face with the French commander.

Accordingly, leaving New York March 2nd, with two aides and General Howe as companions, Washington proceeded (over very bad roads) on horseback to Rhode Island. He reached Conanicut by way of the ferry at about two o'clock in the afternoon, March 6th. All Newport was on tiptoe with expectation. The French officers especially were most anxious to behold their Commander-in-Chief, the great Washington, whose name inspired everywhere such respect and veneration.

The Admiral's barge was in waiting at the Jamestown shore, to convey General Washington to the French flagship, the "Duc de Bourgogne." Here he was received by all the French officers with most distinguished honors. Proceeding thence to the town, he landed at Long Wharf, and escorted by the officers, proceeded up the Parade. The entire body of French troops, all in new uniforms, was drawn up on either side of the way, three deep, as far as the State House, where they formed a right angle, continning the same formation through Clarke Street to the French General's quarters. Rochambeau, unbonneted, walked at the Chief's left, the French nobles and officers, *chapeau bras*, followed in the rear. The firing of the French ships, at the moment of arrival, was tremendous; the solid earth trembled. Washington's honors were those of a Marshal of France, a position which his contemporaries claimed for him, but for which there is now no documentary evidence. He could hardly have commanded all these men of high rank without some recognized authority from their sovereign. Perhaps the title was a complimentary one; Washington disclaimed it later in life, yet we are told by an eye witness that he wore on this occasion the insignia of that rank.

So brilliant was the scene that the populace, crowding roofs, windows and all points of vantage, divided their attention between the gallant allies and the guest of honor.

"Every Frenchman, however, had his eyes directed to Washington. Calm and unmoved by all the honors that surrounded him, the voice of adulation had never disturbed the equanimity of his deportment." A deep impression was made on the onlookers by the attitudes of the nobles, their deep obeisance, the lifting of hats and caps, the waving of standards, and the sea of plumes. "It was a proud day for Newport," says one who was there and saw it all. Proceeding up the living lane of troops, and turning through Clarke Street, the brilliant company disappeared from the view of the spectators within the doors of the Vernon house.

That evening the fleet was dressed with lanterns. Again there was an illumination in the town, the poor but patriotic being provided with candles as before. A procession was formed to go through the streets. Thirty boys led the way, bearing candles fixed to staves. Then came Washington and Rochambeau, followed by the officers and other citizens. It is recorded that on their return to headquarters, Washington, remaining on the steps until the other officers had gone in, personally thanked the boys for their escort—an honor which they were not likely to forget.

That night Rochambeau entertained at supper in Washington's honor. Blanchard, who was present, notes that he marks this as a fortunate day on which he has been able to meet a man so truly great. The impression made on all the French officers was of the happiest; they praise his "easy and noble bearing" and find in him "the art of making himself beloved." Count Mathieu Dumas says of his first meeting with Washington, "We were eager to see the hero of Liberty. His noble bearing, the simplicity of his manners and his gentle gravity surpassed our

CHINA USED BY ROCHAMBEAU DURING HIS STAY IN THE VERNON HOUSE

expectations, and gained him all the French hearts." We may well suppose that on this joyful occasion the healths went round right merrily, the Americans drinking to the King of France, the Frenchmen to the success of the American cause, as their custom was. Washington's uniform tact and social ease must have showed to advantage in the brilliant company which on this night graced the old Vernon house; and this occasion is perhaps the most noteworthy of its history, when America's greatest man and the noble and ardent champions of its cause met beneath this hospitable roof.

It is traditional that the room where Washington slept was the north-west one, over the parlor, and hither we may imagine him marshalled with lights by the major of the household. The costume of this functionary has been preserved to us, and must have been imposing, consisting, as it did, of a silver fringed coat, short close jacket, pink shoes, and a cane with an enormous head.

On the following morning a committee from the Town Council waited on Washington, and presented an address of welcome. They speak in the address of the "happiness the town has enjoyed with the army and fleet of our illustrious ally, who have, by the wisdom and prudence of their commander, as well as their own most zealous inclinations, allied themselves to us not only as soldiers, but as friends and citizens." Washington, who never lost an opportunity to express his appreciation of the aid the French allies were extending to his country, said in his reply: "The conduct of the French army and fleet, of which the inhabitants testify so grateful and so affectionate a sense, at the same time that it evinces the wisdom of the commander and the discipline of the troops, is a new proof of the magnanimity of the nation. It is a further demonstration of that generous zeal and concern for the happiness of America which brought them to our assistance, a happy presage of future harmony."

On the same night, a ball was given in the "French Hall" in honor of the distinguished guest. It is said that as Washington stepped on the floor with his selected partner, the French officers took the instruments from the musicians, and played the music of the dance "A Successful Campaign" as a compliment and omen of future good.

Washington remained in Newport until the 13th of March and was largely entertained. He witnessed a review of the troops, visited Conanicut on the Sunday and, it is said, had a second ball given in his honor. Doubtless he and Rochambeau held high conclave in the north parlor, settling between them the details of campaigns soon to take place. The day after his arrival, the fleet sailed, carrying with them twelve hundred and fifty men of the land forces, under the command of the Chevalier de Viomenil, Rochambeau remaining behind for the time to guard the stores and defenses.

One more story of Washington seems to connect itself with the Vernon House. It is said that a little boy of the town had been very anxious to see the great general. His father, seeing Washington stand near an open window, lifted the child in his arms so that he might get a view of him. Much surprised, the little boy exclaimed, "Why, father, General Washington is a man!" Washington heard him, and, turning, said, "Yes, my lad, and nothing but a man."

On the 13th, Washington took his departure, by way of the Island and Bristol Ferry. He was again treated with the highest honors. Broad Street, far beyond "the head of the town" was lined with troops, the general officers were stationed in the centre, and from Tammany Hill thirteen guns were fired as a salute. Rochambeau rode with him a part of the way, and then turned back, while Washington attended by other of the French officers, passed on, on his way to Providence.

The fleet was, unfortunately, not altogether successful in its sea fight off the Chesapeake, and was obliged to return to Newport. This they did on the 28th of March, having inflicted considerable injury on the enemy.

Early in May, young Rochambeau arrived with supplies of money and the promise of ships, and also with new orders giving his father a much more free hand in his campaigning. Rochambeau at once prepared for action. The heavy artillery here was transferred to Providence; orders were issued that the troops be put in readiness for the field, and one more conference was held with Washington at Wethersfield. A farewell dinner took place on the "Duc de Bourgogne," June 7th, and on the 10th, Rochambeau embarked his army for Providence, leaving only a small guard of 600 men over the stores which remained and the works. On August 25th, the last act in the drama took place, when de Barras, now in command of the fleet, sailed for the Chesapeake. The French occupation was at an end.

Newport saw Rochambeau no more, but it may not be amiss to recall here something of his later career. Loaded with honors on his return from the American campaign, he was made Governor of Picardie and Artois, and later Marshal of France. Condemned to death under the Terror, he was only saved from the guillotine by the fact that the cart into which he was about to mount was full. The man in charge, said to have been one of his old sergeants, said to him, "Withdraw, old Marshal, thy turn will soon come." It never came, however, as the fall of Robespierre followed immediately after, and all the executions were stopped. Living to a good old age, praised by Napoleon, pensioned and an officer of the Legion of Honor, Rochambeau passed his last years in calm retirement, respected and honored by all.

During the year that the French commander occupied his house, William Vernon remained in Boston. His son, Samuel, was, for a part of the time, at least in Newport. Though Mr. Vernon had allowed the use of his house, he seems to have been somewhat disturbed by his son's account of the injury done the dwelling by a "military family."

Samuel Vernon, writing October, 1780, says, "I believe the General takes as much care of the house as the French men generally do, but it will sustain more damage than a family living in it seven years. The Floors will be entirely spoiled." William Vernon says in reply, November, 1780, " I expect they will make a great waste in the house, if not ruin it," and adds that he shall send in a bill for the damage done. This he did, and it is still extant. It was duly honored. It is worthy of notice that no rent is charged, only the cost of necessary repairs.

"His Most Christian Majesty, To W. Vernon, Dr.
1782 To damages sustained in his house at Newport, R. I., occupied by his Excellency Gen'l Rochambeau, viz: Floors, Wainscot, Hangings, Paint, Windows, Walls, Marble Hearths, and in the House and Building throughout: To be made good by the promise of Mr. Corné by agreement 450 dollars, value in L. M.   £135.0.0
To one year's rent of same   000.0.0
Errors excepted. Lawful Money   £135.0.0
Boston, 12 December, 1782.
                      WM. VERNON."

On the back of the paper is the following receipt:

> "Received the full consideration of the above account by the order of His Excellency General Rochambeau.
>
> WM. VERNON."

Rochambeau, his American campaigning at an end, was at this date on his way to Annapolis, to embark for France. His army, under command of the Baron de Viomenil, was, however, newly arrived at Boston, and it was this opportunity that Mr. Vernon embraced to have his bill honored. A few days later, the whole fleet set sail, to join no more in the American struggle for Liberty.

It was fortunate that Vernon's damages were made good in good French livres, for by that time the Continental money had become only so much waste paper. Even in 1780 the French had noted that "it takes sixty piastres to make one in silver," and by the middle of 1781, the currency was at 700 per cent discount; or in other words, seven hundred paper dollars would buy only a dollar's worth of goods. We need not wonder that bundles of paper money of the Continental issue remained in the Vernon House, and remain in the possession of the descendants to this day, valuable now only as curiosities.

William Vernon must now have thought of returning to his home. The Navy Board was settling up its accounts in this year, after much and valuable service to the nation. It may be presumed that His Most Christian Majesty's payment of 450 dollars was of great use in the repairs which were now actively put in progress.

The Floors, the Hangings, the Paint and the Marble Hearths all evidently needed attention. We know from a letter of Samuel Vernon's to his father at about this time how they painted the house—with white lead, with a little red mixed with it, making presumably a pinkish color. Sand was thrown on at the time of painting to give a rough appearance resembling blocks of stone.

At this time also, Samuel conceived the idea of buying the lot opposite the house for a garden. There was an old house on it, which had been damaged by fire and was uninhabitable. If this were removed there would be a clear view to the water. His father concurring, Samuel purchased the lot in 1782 of Myers Fisher, gentleman, of Philadelphia, for 280 Spanish milled dollars. His wife, a Redwood, had it from her grandfather, Samuel Holmes. The old house was removed, and a flower garden laid out here, whose long straight path, with box edgings and flower beds on either side, is still recalled.

In 1784 "Samuel the younger" married his cousin, Miss Betsy Ellery. She it was, who, as a young girl, received General Washington at her father's house. Noticing that she had a heavy cold, he mentioned that he knew of an efficacious though disagreeable cure. The young lady, of course, promised to take anything that General Washington should suggest, when he informed her that his remedy, which he "had often taken," was onions boiled in molasses! Miss Betsey heroically underwent the treatment, and was cured.

Samuel Vernon was, like his father, a merchant, and, it is to be presumed, assisted him in his affairs while residing with him in the Vernon house. In 1785 we find William Vernon in Newport again, once more prepared to engage in commerce, and do his share in building up the prosperity of the discouraged little town. It was fortunate that this one, at least, of our old mercantile families was not permanently driven away by the war. William Vernon was instrumental in founding the Newport Bank, and on the death of the first president of the Redwood Library—Abraham Redwood—was made President in his stead. The old house was now newly set in order, its ancient furnishings once more in place, the long-buried silver restored to the light of day, and family life again going on there.

Samuel Vernon had no less than ten children, all born during his father's life time, and we can imagine the halls again resounding to childish voices, while little feet climb the twisting stairs, and a large and merry company assembles in the cheerful dining room. So lived William Vernon, true type of Revolutionary patriot and man of probity and honor, and here he died in 1806, full of years and respected by all his associates, a worthy son of old Newport.

Samuel Vernon, the younger, was now the head of the house. A solid man, as his father had been before him, he filled a large place in the life of the town. It is said that he was at one time considered the richest man in Newport. He owned houses and land in many parts of the town, the duck factory on the burying ground, and in addition, much property elsewhere, amounting in all to a very large estate. He was the President of the Newport Bank which had been founded by his father, and, actively pursuing his business, once more Vernon ships left Newport harbor to journey over seas, bringing home merchandise of many sorts—fine china, wines and silks.

William Vernon had, as will be remembered, another son, William, often called William H., to distinguish him from his father. The H. probably stands for Harwood, his mother's maiden name. We left young William in Bordeaux, established in the house of a respectable merchant, and engaged in learning the rudiments of business and mastering the French language.

Americans were at this time very much the fashion in France, and young Vernon had the entree to the best society of the capital, through Mr. Adams and Dr. Franklin. He found the life there very much to his taste, and it was long years before his native land saw him again. Handsome and distinguished, with fine manners, it is said that he was a prominent figure at the court of Louis XVI., and a special favorite of Marie Antoinette. His beautiful court suit has been preserved, and is still in the possession of the family. It is of peach colored silk brocade, coat and trousers—while the three waistcoats that belong with it, are of white, embroidered in the same color as the coat. During the terrible Revolution which followed ours, he was in great danger as an aristocrat, and, it is said, was once seized by an infuriated mob, who were on the point of stringing him up to the nearest lamp-post, when a passer-by recognized him as an American, and obtained his release.

Still William Vernon lingered on, and it was not until after the fairest of heads had been laid on the block, and that brilliant society which he had so enjoyed was no more, did he return to his native land. This was in 1796, and a touching picture has been preserved to us of the long absent son, entering his father's house and kneeling to receive his blessing, which was given in true patriarchal style. Henceforth William Harwood Vernon resided in Newport. So much of a Frenchman had he become in his long stay abroad, and so elegant and courteous were his manners that he was commonly called " Count " Vernon— behind his back, be it said.

COURT SUIT WORN BY WILLIAM H. VERNON AT THE COURT OF LOUIS XVI

A story is told of a stranger who, supposing this to be really his title, kept addressing him as "Count" Vernon, "Count" Vernon. Mr. Vernon at last turned on him and said, "Are you a Duke or a Marquis that you give other people titles?" Very fond of flowers, he delighted in aiding his friends in their labors in this direction, showing them how to hybridize pinks in the French fashion, and vying with them in this charming occupation. He was for long the Secretary of the Redwood Library, but perhaps the most interesting thing about him is his well-known and, in its day, famous, collection of pictures.

On his return from France "Count" Vernon had brought with him what was considered a remarkable collection of paintings, attributed to the first masters of that or any age. It is difficult to say, now that they are lost to sight, whether they were genuine originals in every case, but it is certain that in the disorganization and confusion of Revolution, many fine collections were broken up in France, and the opportunity was unrivalled for securing masterpieces. "Count" Vernon's own list is in existence of these pictures—fifty-six in number they were. He says that he only names those which he knows to be by the masters given. If his authorities were to be depended on, he had a most valuable collection. These were examples of Canaletti's work and Paolo Veronesi's; pictures by Murillo and Van Dyke, while Claude Lorraine, Mignard and Vernet were also represented. Mr. Vernon exhibited a selection from these pictures during his life-time at the Boston Athenaeum. This was in 1830. He evidently felt somewhat nervous for their safety. They were despatched on brig "Ivory" and were insured for $10,000, which he said was not nearly their real value. The vessel being "a fast sailer, coppered to the bends, well appointed and merely in a good set of ballast" accomplished her journey successfully, and the patrons of the Athenaeum doubtless much enjoyed the exhibition. The "Saint Rock, presented by one of the Popes to the Cathedral at Thoulouse—a masterly production of a masterly hand," was among these, as was the "Dying Seneca" by Van Dyke ("the genius of the artist is in the expression of this painting, which follows us to our closet") and the "Laughing Boy, a picture which would honor the gallery of the Louvre or Florence," by Girardo della Notti. William H. Vernon died in 1833. His pictures were two years later put up at auction in Newport, and sold for pitifully small sums, considering the value he put upon them. The prices seem to have ranged, (judging by the catalogue, still extant, with pencilled memoranda,) from twenty, thirty or fifty dollars, to, in case of the Van Dyke, three hundred. Only one other brought so high a figure as this, and that was bid in by the family, as were several others.

This picture listed as "A Nun, a finished piece, by Leonardo da Vinci," has aroused special interest of late years. It is a beautiful painting, nearly a perfect replica of the famous "Mona Lisa." In William Vernon's own list of his pictures, the price that he paid for them is mentioned in every case, save that of the "Nun," and it is the cherished tradition of the family that this especial painting was presented to him by Marie Antoinette. It is certain that he had a special regard for this picture, keeping it in his own room, and, it is said, being sometimes found on his knees before it. The Vernon "Mona Lisa" was many years ago taken to the Louvre and hung beside the French "Mona Lisa," where it is said that the critics were unable to see any perceptible difference between

THE VERNON MONA LISA

them. As is well known, there is a tradition that there were three "Mona Lisa's" painted, one of them being in Madrid, one in the Louvre; the whereabouts of the third being unknown. It is, perhaps, too much to hope that this should be the lost exemplar, but it is at all events a fine piece of work and of especial interest, on account of its curious story. It is still retained in the Vernon family.

Samuel Vernon died the year after his brother in 1834. His widow lived on in the old house, not dying until 1857.

Their youngest son, Samuel Brown Vernon, now occupied the property. Born in 1802, he married in 1830, Sophia Peace, the daughter of a Philadelphia gentleman. They had five children, Joseph Peace, Thomas, Ellery, Anna and Elizabeth. Mr. Vernon was a most kindly, amiable gentleman, rather retiring and quiet. He was for long State Treasurer. A miniature by Inman in the possession of the family, shows his scholarly and thoughtful face and slight build. The delightful family life of this time is still recalled—the old house filled with charming, old-fashioned furniture, the delightful entertainments, the gay Virginia reels extending the length of the hall, the musical daughter with her piano—the picture is a most attractive one. The figure of Mr. Vernon, slender and abstracted, is remembered, pacing in the garden, between his rows of Indian corn, on which he specially prided himself, while the charming little mistress of the house and her sister, Mrs. Horner, sit one on either side of the fireplace, like two dainty Dresden china images. It is sad to think that the house was soon to be a "Vernon house" in name only. Mr. Vernon died in 1858, only a year after his mother. In the late sixties the family went abroad. It seemed probable that they would return no more to Newport, and in 1872 the house was sold and the furniture scattered at an auction sale. The house and land were bought by Mr. Harwood E. Read. For a time the house stood empty or was rented. In 1876, the estate was broken up, the Spring Street frontage being sold in part to Mr. Franklin, who built his brick bakery there. Mr. Barker's paint shop occupies the rest. On Clarke Street a good sized lot was sold, the site of the "French Hall" and stable. The garden across the street was later sold to Mrs. Pell, of the old Cheseborough house across Mary Street.

In 1879 and for several years the Vernon house was used as offices by the United States Geological Survey, under the direction of Mr. Raphael Pumpelly. During this time a "large and broad panel" was taken out over a fireplace, and behind it was found a curious old painting on plaster, three feet by three and a half. It seemed to represent a scene in the West Indies. There were ladies with guitars, a castle, and blackamoors holding horses. The frieze above was of passion flowers and sea shells. Paintings over fireplaces were not uncommon in Newport, but were usually hunting scenes. After the term of the Geological Survey, Mr. Read himself lived in the house.

Twice again the connection of the Vernon house with Rochambeau is recalled. The first of these occasions is in 1902. Not long before this time a statue of the Count had been erected in Vendôme, his native place. A movement was set on foot to secure a replica of this statue for America. It was pointed out, that, while there were six or seven statues of the Marquis de Lafayette in the United States, Rochambeau was nowhere commemorated in this way; although he was the Commander-in-Chief of the French forces, thus typifying the official intervention of the King of France in American affairs.

The suggestion was warmly taken up and a sum of $90,000 appropriated by Congress for the statue and the purchase of a site in Washington, etc. The Committee to whom the bill was referred, have this to say of Rochambeau: "He was a great and noble man. His deeds deserve to be remembered by all generations of our countrymen, and his heroic personality ever recalled to us and our children, forever, in enduring bronze; for to him and his military ability, as well as to the brave and willing sons of France he commanded, in an important degree we owe the fact of our independence as a nation."

The date of the unveiling of the statue was set for May 24th, 1902, and an invitation was extended to the government and people of France, and especially to the families of Rochambeau and Lafayette, to be present. A warship was sent over from France to bring prominent officers of the Army and Navy, and a number of other persons, distinguished in diplomacy, letters and art, also came over especially for the occasion.

The statue is a fine one. It is of heroic size and represents Rochambeau in the uniform of his rank. His arm is extended in a gesture of command. At the base of the statue is the bronze figure of Liberty, stepping from a boat as it first touches the shores of America. She grasps in her hand the combined colors of the two countries.

The ceremony of unveiling the statue was a success in every respect, and on May 31st, the delegates, by direction of President Loubet of France, proceeded to Newport, to lay a wreath on the tomb of de Ternay, the associate of Rochambeau. The foreign guests were more than twenty in number, and included Réné, Comte de Rochambeau, the present head of the family, and a representative of the name of Lafayette, Comte Salume de Lafayette. On arriving in Newport, the French delegates were escorted by the Artillery Company, in a route that passed the Vernon house, to Trinity Church. On the steps of the old house were a number of little boys and girls in white, with French flags, which they waved, shouting "Vive la France." The little granddaughter of Mr. Read was held up to the side of the carriage of the present Count de Rochambeau, to present him with a bouquet of white roses—a gift which he acknowledged with a kiss.

Later in the day, the distinguished visitors, by their special request, returned to the Vernon house, and were shown over the house and entertained there, thus agreeably linking the present with the past.

The other interesting occasion was in September, 1908, when a bronze tablet in memory of Rochambeau was affixed to the house. This tablet was presented by the "Alliance Francaise," a society of persons interested in French belles-lettres, etc. At the unveiling a notable company of persons was gathered. The Count de Chambrun, counsellor of the French embassy at Washington and a lineal descendant of Lafayette, made an address, and Mrs. Julia Ward Howe pulled the ribbons which released the tricolor covering the tablet. The Newport Artillery fired a salute and the Training Station band played the Marseillaise. The Mayor of Newport, accepting the tablet in behalf of the citizens of the town, said: "It has been the custom for centuries to commemorate men of valor by inscriptions in bronze, as we are doing today, in order to perpetuate and accentuate the lives of such men. There is but one other way that fitting tribute may be paid to such a man as Count de Rochambeau, and that is the lasting record of gratitude, deep seated in the memories of those he came to aid, and, by them, transmitted a lasting

**ROCHAMBEAU TABLET ON THE
VERNON HOUSE**

acknowledgment through generation after generation. Rochambeau and Lafayette are enshrined in every American heart with Greene and Washington."

The tablet is a medallion portrait of the Count de Rochambeau in green bronze, and represents him as he appeared when in Newport, at the age of 58. The likeness was the result of much research and study on the part of the sculptor, M. Pierre de Feitu, a Frenchman residing in New York.

The last chapter in the history of the Vernon house now remains to be told. In 1912, Mr. Read, for so long its owner, died, and the property was for sale. The Charity Organization Society of Newport was very anxious to find a suitable home. The idea occurred to members of the Society that if the Vernon house could be purchased for this purpose, it would be most suitable for them, and also the means of preserving unchanged one of our finest old houses. An appeal was sent out to members and friends for a fund of ten thousand dollars. Very generous responses followed, from interested summer visitors, Newporters both here and away, and representatives of old families as such, of Newport and on the island. The Newport Daily News aided the good work by publishing the lists of donations day by day, and in a surprisingly short time the object was accomplished, and the house secured for $6,500. The heirs of Mr. Read were much interested in the project, and aided by kindly giving an extension of time and in other ways. A thorough renovation was now in order. The old front door and sash of the stair window were found in the attic and replaced; a modern door to the south was taken out and a window put in its place, as originally arranged, and all the panelling and woodwork put in good order. The old brass knocker is on the door, the old lantern that long hung above the door, was presented by a friend. The large iron lock on the front door is from the old Bull house, the oldest in the State, recently destroyed by fire. The interior detail and finish remain untouched, save for needed repairs. Walls were scraped and painted and all woodwork painted white, while the floors were finished in green with the old-fashioned " spatter-dash." The small space to the east of the house is planted with old-time flowers, recalling its earlier days as part of the garden. The second story of the house has been fitted up as a dwelling, while the two south rooms on the ground floor are arranged for offices, leaving the north or Washington room for occasional use.

Thus preserved, beautified and cherished, the old house bids fair to delight the eyes and inspire the patriotism of generations yet to come. Long may it stand as a worthy memorial of merchant, patriot, chief and generous ally—its past inextricably entertwined with Newport's, its memories enriched with the names of Bowler, Vernon, Rochambeau and Washington, its present use, one diguified and altogether worthy—the Vernon house, Newport's pride, an object of pilgrimage and study.

No house could present more fully an epitome of Newport's history; we count ourselves fortunate in its preservation, and hope for it a long life of continued usefulness.